Guest Rooms

Guest Rooms

AND PRIVATE PLACES

Anna Kasabian

PRINCIPAL PHOTOGRAPHY BY Shelley Metcalf

contributing photographers:

MICHEL ARNAUD, KINDRA CLINEFF, MICHAEL GRIMM, ANNA KASABIAN,

DAVID KASABIAN, NANCY KLEMM, ERIC ROTH, JAMIE SALOMON, VICENTE WOLF

UNIVERSE

First published in the
United States of America
in 2005
by UNIVERSE PUBLISHING
A Division of Rizzoli International
Publications, Inc.
300 Park Avenue South
New York, NY 10010
www.rizzoliusa.com

© 2005 by Anna Kasabian

2005 2006 2007
10 9 8 7 6 5 4 3 2 1

Printed in China

ISBN: 0-7893-1305-7

Library of Congress Catalog Control
Number: 2004117712

For my late mother, Katie, and my husband, David

Contents

Preface

~~~~~~

Since childhood I have been intrigued with other people's homes and the private places within them, especially the bedrooms. As a lifestyle editor many years ago, I found myself looking for stories about houses and their gardens, particularly grand, old homes that bookmarked times like the Gilded Age.

But it was a press conference I attended back then that would forever glue me to this topic. A special announcement was being made by Mine Crane in the magnificent library of her family's summer mansion in Ipswich, Massachusetts. Her father-in-law, Richard Crane of the Chicago-based plumbing empire, had built an amazing house on a hill overlooking a stunning white powdery beach that wraps the shoreline. Ms. Crane was announcing that an additional seven hundred acres of land (including Hog Island, where her husband Cornelius was buried), would be given to the preservation group called the Trustees of Reservations. I stepped into this beautiful old summer home, called the Crane mansion at Castle Hill, and

Here is one of the guest rooms at Castle Hill. Guests who woke here could look out to the rolling lawn, lined with statues, that leads to the sea and beach below. Owned by Chicago plumbing millionaire Richard T. Crane, Jr., the estate included farm buildings, gardens, designed grounds, and natural areas, and came to characterize the American "Country Place Era." Some of the century's most notable architects and landscape architects made its grounds a visual extravaganza of color, texture, and magnificent views. Crane and his family would come here every summer on a private train from Chicago. Today the house is open to tours and the vast beach is open to the public.

Views from the bedroom on page x.

ABOVE: *One of two guest pavilions at Castle Hill, built in 1914–1916.*

OPPOSITE: *The maid and valet calling buttons are located on the bed stand in this bedroom at Castle Hill.*

Called the Belfray Chamber, this guest bedroom is located in Beauport, once the summer home and weekend escape of Boston's Henry David Sleeper, one of America's most talented interior designers, a pioneer decorator, and a trendsetter. Described as a "veritable labyrinth," the home, which sits on the edge of the ocean in Gloucester, Massachusetts, has more than forty rooms. Built for entertaining guests, the house is filled with Sleeper's playful compositions of thousands of decorative art objects.

The guests who were lucky enough to stay here reached this particular room via a staircase that curls upward from behind a hidden door in the room below.

was awestruck by the remarkable details of the room and the stunning view of the rolling lawn to the sea.

From New York's Hudson River Valley mansions to the Berkshires, this, and other historically significant homes like the Stevens-Coolidge Place in North Andover, Massachusetts, or Beauport in Gloucester, provided guests with romantic, often luxurious escapes. They were summer homes that hosted guests who came for weekends by steamship or the new railroad that had cut its way north. Guest rooms were thoughtfully located within the homes and situated to take advantage of the pretty views of walking paths, kitchen cutting gardens, and rose gardens.

What dreamy places to be a guest! These homes signified a lifestyle we will not see as guests or hosts in this century. Neither can we ever duplicate such extraordinary places.

As my writing assignments and travels took me to new places, from inns and old resorts to family homes where I was a guest, the thought kept surfacing that it is the rooms we stay in, the internal pathways to reach them, and the views within them, that add the most dimension to the mental scrapbooks from our travels. And the smallest of details in those rooms stick with us as well: the antique leather-bound book on butterflies we thumbed through one morning, or the pile of sea glass that glimmered in the light.

Of all the public places I have stayed in as a guest, my very favorite was the Westways Inn on Kezar Lake in Maine, which was once the summer home of the owner of the Diamond Match Company. Before it went back to being a private home, I managed to stay in several rooms there, but my absolute favorite was called the master bedroom. It was paneled in dark wood, furnished simply, and had a magnificent view of the lake. The bathroom was big and had a deep claw-foot tub that was irresistible. When the windows were open, the sound of the loon's cry could lull me into a nap. There was nothing fancy in here. The screened boathouse perched above the lake, just steps away, had nothing in it except for a row of wonderful old green wicker chairs. When the sun set over the lake, the purple-pink of the sky would wash across its wood floor like a magical tide.

The facade of the Stevens-Coolidge Place.

One of two guest bedrooms at the Stevens-Coolidge Place. This one takes in the views of the garden.

Views of the Stevens-Coolidge Place, North Andover, the summer home of Boston residents John Gardner Coolidge and Helen Stevens Coolidge from 1914 to 1962. Mr. Coolidge was a diplomat and a descendant of Thomas Jefferson. The home, formerly known as Ashdale Farm, belonged to Helen's family, and with her husband's support, she transformed the farm into an elegant agricultural estate that exemplified gracious country living. Guests who came here could enjoy the home and its outdoor spaces, which included a perennial garden, a kitchen and cut-flower garden, a rose garden, and a French potager garden with brick serpentine wall.

S·S·PIERCE·Co·

Established 1831   Incorporated 1894.   135 #2

·IMPORTERS·&·GROCERS·

BOSTON,   August 1911

old to

Mr J G Coolidge

386 Beacon St.,

Boston

	AMOUNT.
Brought Forward	33 94
1 Box Self Fitting Sandles	1 32
4 Rd Cans Salmon	1 00
½ Bbl Flour	3 55
¼ ℔ Box Jamaica Ginger	15
¼ ℔ Box Nutmegs	25
¼ ℔ Box Cloves	15
¼ ℔ Box Cassia	25
½ Pint Vanilla	95
2 oz Bot Lemon Ext	18
5℔ Bag Salt	08
1 Box Swansdowne Salt	10
1 Peck Rock Salt	18

LEFT: *A grocery list that hangs in the kitchen at the Stevens–Coolidge Place, perhaps in preparation for dinner guests.*

OPPOSITE: *The dining room at the Stevens–Coolidge Place, set as though breakfast guests were on their way.*

The Mount, from the walled garden. Photograph by Kevin Sprague, courtesy of Edith Wharton Restoration.

There was a lesson here, one that Emily Post summarized in her 1930 book, *The Personality of a House:*

> At all events, it makes not the least difference in the world whether the interior decoration of a spare room be elaborate and its furniture of fabulous value, or whether its walls be whitewashed and the entire contents of the room have no intrinsic value at all. But there is one requirement that cannot be overlooked, and that is its comfort, its convenience, judged by the standards of its occupants.

So what is it that really makes the perfect guest room? It is, I think, all about the experience of the place and its people. As Berkely Updike, a frequent guest at Edith Wharton's the Mount, said: "The Mount was a delightful house to stay in, 'not a bit sophisticated in its atmosphere—full of gaiety and fun of a very simple sort: we laughed until we cried." (*The Mount, Home of Edith Wharton* by Edith Wharton Restoration, Inc., 1997.)

Can we live happily in a guest room without the perfect reading chair? Can it be made of wicker, and be a little wobbly? Without a writing table? Yes. But if, as hosts and hostesses, we can accommodate some of these simple pleasures, while giving our spaces a cheerful theme, we have done a good thing. And don't forget good food and lively dialogue to provide your guests with fond memories of their stay.

Throughout this book you will see many quotes written about the Mount, the summer home of writer Edith Wharton and her husband Teddy in Lenox, Massachusetts. Lenox was at one time referred to as the "inland Newport," a getaway for the wealthy, who traveled by rail from the surrounding cities. Ms. Wharton was, by all accounts, the quintessential hostess who not only created a beautiful country home here, but gave her guests delightful, memorable experiences. These quotes, juxtaposed to stories that reflect modern times, capture the spirit of a successful host-guest experience. Yes, times have changed, but the joy of bringing comfort and tranquility to a home full of guests remains the same.

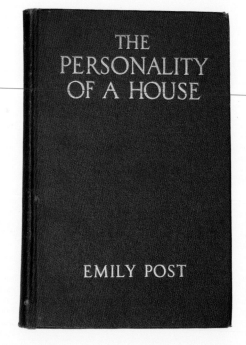

Introduction

~~~~~~

No matter what the size, a guest room is a home within a home, a place to relax, tend to normal tasks, and eventually sink into a peaceful, undisturbed sleep.

The bed we sleep in, or the desk we write a note on, may have once had another life in the family, which can make this place even more special. How moving is it to sleep in what once was the bridal bed of our host and hostess, or the bed a little girl grew up in? One hostess I spoke with chooses to share the stories behind the furnishings in her guest room by leaving a short handwritten explanation on a card. For hosts and hostesses, the guest room can also be a creative outlet—a place to bring art, fabric, color, and design details together in new, even unexpected ways.

Guest spaces are sometimes planned for when homes are being built or redesigned; they may be in the main house or in a separate, smaller cottage. Today architects are transforming all kinds of outbuildings into private guest cottages, from stables to pool houses, as well as creating new structures for guests. They may recall the style of the main house, or be built in a style a family has a passion for, such as the teahouse on page 110.

In the 1914 book *The House in Good Taste,* written by America's self-proclaimed "first lady of interior decoration," Elsie de Wolfe noted that the best guest bedrooms were small, highly

OPPOSITE: *The cover of Emily Post's book.*

personalized spaces that included "a comfortable bed with a small table beside it to hold a reading light, a clock, and a telephone; a chaise lounge for resting; a long mirror somewhere; a dressing table with proper lights and a glass-covered top; a writing table, carefully equipped, and the necessary chairs and stools."

Her design advice certainly rings true today. As you peruse this book it's not likely you will pass a guest room without these basics in some form. The simple one-hundred-year-old lake cabin in Canada has the same features as the high-styled Puerto Vallarta seaside getaway.

De Wolfe's comment that "nothing so nice happened in a long time as the revival of painted furniture, and the application of quaint designs to modern beds and chairs and chests," is also as relevant today as it was then. Some ninety years later, painting furniture is back in fashion, as are white metal beds, which she believed then would have lasting power. Evidence of this can be found in the Diamond Island, Maine, and Manchester-by-the-Sea projects, among others.

In Emily Post's book *The Personality of a House*, her ten-point list of requirements to achieve "guest room perfection" can be applied to any modern-day guest space. Take a look:

1. A bathroom of its own
2. A delightful bed
3. Plenty of air and light
4. Choice of pillows
5. A good light to read by in bed
6. Heat in cold weather
7. Cross-ventilation in hot weather
8. A sofa to rest on
9. Situation as free from noise as possible

She describes the delightful bed as one with a thick, spongy mattress, and warm, light blankets. No need, she says, for silk sheets or even linen. Cotton is just fine; just make sure it is soft, quality cotton.

If there is room for a dressing table, she says, situate it in good natural light during the day and make sure to set a table lamp on it for adequate light at night. She also advises that you leave its surface open so guests can put down their personal items.

Her other suggestions include:

* A writing table that has everything a guest needs to write, including pens, paper, stamps, scissors, and a pad
* A sofa with pillows and a quilt
* Blinds that keep the room dark
* "Eye bandages"
* Books—best-sellers, go-to-sleep essays "on topics that are not too absorbing," a book of short stories, and magazines

In discussing the guest bathroom, Post offers a design recipe that includes a tub and shower, a big medicine-closet, mirrors, a big window, a chair, towels, and plenty of heat in the cold weather.

"IT IS THE DAY OF OUR DEPARTURE, ALAS! FROM THIS HEAVENLY PLACE, WHICH

WE HAVE SEEN FOR THE FIRST TIME, UNDER THE BEST OF AUSPICES—THE

AFFECTIONATE HOSPITALITY OF AN OLD FRIEND WHO UNITES CARE FOR THE

BODY WITH NOURISHMENT FOR THE MIND."

—Matilda Gay, diary entry about a visit to Ste.-Claire-le-Château, quoted in William Rieder, "Edith Wharton and the Walter Gays"

CHAPTER ONE

On Island Time

This chapter tours five oceanfront escapes, where the magnificent views of greenery, forest, flowers, and open sea have inspired the spirit of the architecture and interior design.

These are places where the walls of the rooms may recall the color of the sand or the bleached white of a nearby picket fence, and where fabrics, art, and throw rugs reintroduce nature's striking palette. The ocean breezes and the fresh smell of the sea are an integral part of the experience, and windows, shutters, and doorways are designed to take it all in. Rooms are crisp and bright; sheer curtains welcome the light; and smooth stone floors are cool underfoot. Thoughtfully situated patios and hammocks remind guests why they are here.

These places allow guests the ultimate opportunity to unwind. They are not about what we wear, but rather what we don't wear. They are not about keeping to a schedule, but are all about the moment.

Paradise Redux

This island getaway called Frenchman's Lookout seemed to be in the stars for this Cambridge, Massachusetts, family. More than twenty-six years ago Dick Friedman came upon the land where this home now sits. A walk up a logging road with his little boy, Alex, brought him to a site he could never forget, a place he dreamed he would someday live.

Five years ago, when he saw an ad for a home here, he knew by the description of this, the highest point in Frenchman's Cay, that it had to be on that same magical and unforgettable spot. A trip to the island proved him right. The fact that the long-uninhabited home needed quite a bit of work, both inside and out, was incidental to Dick, who develops real estate for a living. He could easily see beyond the garish paint choices, the sad state of the kitchen, and the thick layer of moss and slime in the pool.

He and his wife, Nancy, decided this would be the perfect winter escape for themselves; their toddler son, Jake; and their friends, from Hollywood stars to politicians; as well as for Dick's now grown son, Alex. With a crew of thirty workmen, the home was cleaned and painted in just three months, and the Friedmans left the winter chill behind for their first December vacation here.

Guests have their choice of hammocks to enjoy the views.

The house sits two hundred and fifty feet above the Sir Francis Drake Channel at the southwestern tip of Frenchman's Cay, offering unobstructed 360-degree views of the British Virgin Islands, St. John, Little Thatch, and the picturesque anchorage of Soper's Hole. With no neighbors in site, guests are treated to privacy and peace—and that is the whole idea of being here.

With two floors of wraparound decks, all the rooms open to the ocean and island views with mahogany-carved French doors. Even the guest bathrooms look to the sea; showers are walled-in glass blocks. Terra-cotta floors are cool underfoot and are easy to keep clean no matter how heavy the beach traffic in and out. Wicker, rattan, and sea grass mats top the floors. Modern, comfortable furnishings are covered in cotton fabrics, and a subdued palette of yellows, gold, green, and white makes room for the vibrant colors of the setting. The house came with massive British antique furnishings, many of which the Friedmans decided to keep. Beautifully carved, they fit the scale of the high-ceilinged rooms.

The Friedmans gutted the old kitchen and built out a new one that incorporated simple, Shaker-style cabinetry painted deep green, and granite countertops. It is casual, and welcoming to guests who can come and go as they please. Fresh fruit is plentiful and in bowls, ready for anyone passing to the pool or beach. And fresh flowers from the garden are placed in each of the rooms, which make for enchanting views, both inside and out.

Landscape architect Steve Stimpson of Woods Hole, Massachusetts, worked with a local landscape company to redesign and replant the property. One nice touch was the planting of jasmine, so that when the island winds blow, everyone can enjoy that wonderful sweet smell wafting across the decks and at poolside.

Nancy says that when they do leave their hideaway, it's for brief island-hopping jaunts that take them and their guests to new restaurants or to new snorkeling spots. But her favorite way to spend an evening here is with friends, having a fresh grilled dinner of Caribbean lobster, and then stargazing off the decks. The Friedmans hung five hammocks in different corners of the decks, and added wicker lounge chairs that can be moved to catch the sun or stars.

A blond European armoire that came with the house provides texture and a sunny glow. The symmetry of twin Crate & Barrel lounge chairs separated by a tiny table gives this room a Zen-like calm. With a view to the island of St. John, guests could choose to spend the day right in here.

Simple, no-fuss furnishings: a couch from Crate & Barrel and rattan chairs from Pottery Barn mix with antique African bowls that sit atop a coffee table by renowned architect Charles Gwathmey. Original cruise ship posters that Dick collected wrap the room in punchy colors.

"THE WEATHER IS DELIGHTFULLY COOL, THE COUNTRY IS BEAUTIFUL, & I AM MORE IN LOVE WITH LENOX THAN EVER. WE CAN'T OFFER YOU MANY SOCIAL DIVERSIONS, BUT I CAN SHOW YOU SOME JOLLY BOOKS & CAN MAKE YOUR MOUTH WATER BY DESCRIBING THE (20) WORKS OF ART WE HAVE BROUGHT OUT WITH US."

—Edith Wharton to Ogden Codman, July 10, 1900

No matter which room a guest chooses, the view will be enchanting; the ocean breeze will be plentiful.

Come Undone, Naturally

Situated in Punta Mita, a residential and hotel development where the Bay of Banderas meets the emerald green Pacific just north of Puerto Vallarta, this wonderful escape is nestled on the ninth fairway of the Four Seasons Resort's golf course. It is the first home to be built in the development, and each of its rooms captures the colorful, serene views of this tropical paradise.

The color palette within is inspired by the landscape: sky blue, clay red, and purple. The materials and furnishings recall the natural surroundings, as does the nature-themed fabric used throughout the house. In the powder room, red walls evoke the color of a garden bloom, while the pewter sink is in the shape of a conch shell.

The goal of the design was to feel no boundaries between the inside and outside. The master bedroom is situated so that one view peeks through the arbor to the fairway and off to the ocean, and another looks across the pool to the ocean. Guest bedrooms share similar views, and each has a distinct design, mood, and theme. Many of the design details reflect the owners' love of Mexico. Natural wood shutters open to lush garden views and welcome the ocean breezes, all of which provides guests with the ultimate in pampering and peace.

Guest bedrooms were thoughtfully located so as to open out to the pool and outdoor dining areas.

ABOVE: *This pleasant little red powder room is a mix of old and new, from the whimsical lights to the antique table that holds the pewter conch shell sink.*

OPPOSITE: *Thanks to the imaginative placement of windows, a guest can lie in bed and see the night sky. The owner loves palm trees, so this watercolor-styled fabric on the bedcover was the perfect fit for continuing the indoor/outdoor theme. Both guest room floors are a detailed mix of polished and unpolished marble, keeping the mood casual and the floor cool.*

ABOVE: *Sinking into this little pool for a while would surely help a guest unwind after a long trip. All negative thoughts would vanish once these shutters swing open and let in the sweet floral smells that hang thick in the air.*

OPPOSITE: *Turning down the bed for guests is always a nice touch, as are fresh flowers and an extra pillow. The natural fibered headboard and practical storage bench keep this room comfortable and casual.*

Nestled in Nature's Best

TOFINO VANCOUVER ISLAND, CANADA

Guests who come here have to really want to spend time with the owner. It's a two-hour ferry ride, followed by a four-hour drive to the house. But the drive meanders through ancient-growth forest, beginning the long wind-down for those who come here to relax. When guests arrive, they leave their cars and take a short walk through the woods to the house. Once they get inside, facing the grand expanse of ocean views, the time it took to get here is quickly forgotten.

The house was built on stilts for environmental reasons; it was the only way the construction would avoid damaging the roots of the rainforest growth beneath. But it worked aesthetically as well. Being perched like this, with the trees up close to the house, makes it feel like a tree house.

The house was designed to feel the environment in every way possible—from being sited to take advantage of the views outside to the structure itself, which is made from materials found on the island.

Natural wood is an integral part of the home's design details, both inside and out. Douglas fir floors and wood beams warm the common spaces. The all-white furnishings provide a backdrop to the dramatic views outside, their loose fit casual and comfortable for this island getaway.

The two guest bedrooms are purposely small and sparse in terms of furnishings; after all, no one stays inside while the sun

At the end of a day at the beach, guests can come together here to compare notes on how many eagles they spotted overhead, or the wipeouts they had on their surfboards.

39

is out. Built-ins climb the walls and can accommodate guests for a weekend or week. What is not small or sparse are the views from the guest-room windows—one looks to the ocean and the other to the canopy of trees.

All the bedrooms are on the second floor, and there is an observatory at the very top floor, complete with a telescope for watching shooting stars. All the rooms connect to an open central core, so that guests can meet outside their doors and make plans for a day of surfing or relaxing at the beach. A large, open main living room brings everyone together at the end of the day. It is here that the owner, Terry, most enjoys being—in the place he designed around nature and friendship.

ABOVE: *A wall of colorful built-ins in this guest room eliminates the need for a dresser and invites the casual toss of jeans, sweat-shirts, and bathing suits into the cubbies.*

OPPOSITE: *More than 160 windows capture the dramatic views that surround the house.*

There is no better place to come together for a meal than in a room where the views leave everyone breathless.

"THE REJOICINGS HERE ARE UNBRIDLED. IT IS DEAR OF YOU TO TAKE THAT LONG JOURNEY TO COME [TO THE MOUNT] & CELEBRATE WITH YOUR RUSTIC FRIENDS, & I AM SO GLAD THAT BAY [GEORGE CABOT LODGE] IS COMING TOO. IF I COULD FIND A FAIRY WHO WOULD SUIT YOU BOTH I SHOULD SECURE HER AT ONCE. NAME ONE, & THE WIRES WILL BE HOT IN PURSUIT; BUT REMEMBER, SHE MUST BE NOT ONLY BEAUTIFUL & BAD, BUT ABLE TO BEAR A GOOD DEAL OF COOL WEATHER & OF POETRY IN THE EVENING. TEDDY SAYS WHEN WE ARE ALL TOGETHER THE HOUSE WILL BECOME INCANDESCENT & SULPHUR FUMES RISE THROUGH THE ROOF—& THE 'HOW?' CHIMNEY-POT WILL TURN ITS TRUMPET DOWN THE FLUE IN ITS EAGERNESS TO MISS NOTHING."

—Edith Wharton to Walter Berry, November 15, ca. 1905,

in Evergreen House correspondence file, EWR reference files

Seaside Serenity

OAHU, HAWAII

When you have a house in a place as beautiful as Hawaii, friends and family will come. And sharing it is what it's all about. Suzy and Clint Churchill found their place in the sun back in 1969, and since then, their home has hosted many guests and family members, as well as a dozen weddings. On Kailua Bay on the island of Oahu, their home is steps from the beach, with views that are the stuff of watercolor paintings and Kodak moments.

With so many guests coming and going, Suzy's focus is on simplicity and easy care. She furnished the house with casual, sturdy furnishings and fabrics. Splashes of color come from cotton fabrics, while walls are painted a crisp white. Everything, from bed throws to rugs to slipcovers, has to be washable, she says, since sand, dog hair, and children are part of the lifestyle.

Each guest bedroom has its own bath, and one of the two, which used to be the master bedroom, also has its own patio. Today the new master bedroom is in its own wing of the house, offering privacy to guests and hosts alike.

To let in the incredible trade winds, wide louvers were installed in the main rooms and guest bedrooms, rather than glass. That way, when the rain pours down from a passing cloud, the rooms are filled with the sound and intoxicating smell of drenched island greenery.

Guests can escape beachside with breakfast or a good book.

ABOVE: *This guest bathroom carries the beach theme.*

OPPOSITE: *What used to be the master bedroom is now a guest bedroom with its own patio. A cool stone floor is perfect for this beach house. The bright orange quilt might be replaced with a purple one next month, if the spirit moves Suzy. She uses white as her canvas, and likes to change accents to keep the look fresh and fun.*

A brightly colored quilt, throw rug, and accent pillow reflect the palette just outside the louvered window. Surfboards are a reminder that unwinding is the word of the day.

"I HAVE DRUNK OF THE WINE OF LIFE AT LAST, I HAVE

KNOWN THE THING BEST WORTH KNOWING, I HAVE

BEEN WARMED THROUGH AND THROUGH, NEVER TO

GROW QUITE COLD AGAIN TILL THE END."

—Edith Wharton (source unknown), reprinted by permission of
the Estate of Edith Wharton and the Watkins/Loomis Agency

Friends and family can come together in this great room, which is open to the outdoors. The white-on-white theme seems to automatically lower the temperature.

Endless Views of Blue

BAJA, CALIFORNIA

Patty and Fred first came to Baja on their honeymoon. A passion for deep-sea fishing—waters here are considered the world's richest for sports fishing—brought the couple here, and they stayed in many different hotels over the years. But twelve years ago the couple decided to build a second home in Baja. The plan was to live here six months of the year and enjoy all the area has to offer with their family and friends.

The house is situated on a stunningly beautiful point where the Sea of Cortez meets the Pacific, and where you can clearly see Punta Gordo, which defines the tip of Baja. Designer Ken Ronchetti calls it "intense and dramatic," a place of rocky ledge and twenty-two-foot waves, where hurricanes are not uncommon. For Ronchetti's firm, it was a perfect match. His clients' homes are usually hanging off cliffs, or close to the ocean's edge—"scary sites" as he calls them, but just the type of terrain they love to work with.

To create a picturesque setting that responded to the unique site, the firm designed a series of gardens, including two that crisscross and run down the hillside. They built the home at an angle for a clear view of the sunrise, and created multiple terraces that work their way to the sea. An edgeless pool lies just outside the guest house, perfectly situated so that grandchildren can take a wake-up dip.

Suspended bridges with terra-cotta railings lead guests to their rooms and offer privacy. Each room has its own terrace

Guest rooms open poolside, where there are plenty of lounge chairs to accommodate day and overnight guests.

and bath, decorated with high-fired Mexican tiles. The terraces provide a nice place to nap or read, and offer natural ventilation for the rooms. Screened teak louvers can be closed for privacy or to keep the sun out. Food and wine can be delivered to the guests via a dumbwaiter.

Explaining the design concept as "life in your bathing suit," Ronchetti says the house is meant to feel like a single-family resort. His design inspiration came from a home in Sardinia, Italy. There is a refuge feeling, and it is very quiet.

The house is just steps from the beach, allowing the weather to move swiftly in and out of the rooms. Dampness is common, and so Ronchetti designed the house with concrete inside and out. The floors and walls are concrete, as are the guest bedroom patio benches, the couches, and even the beds. If beach sand gets trailed in, Patty can just pick up the cotton throw rugs and hose the inside clean. Wooden mats are placed under the mattresses to keep them dry.

When it came time to furnish the interior, Patty turned to Robert Schwarzenbach of Los Angeles for advice. Most furniture for the main house came from Kathleen Spiegelman Interiors of West Hollywood. The brightly colored fabrics to accent the guest house came from a local fabric store. The most important element of the décor, however, has been the time the family has spent at this beloved getaway. The lived-in look prevails.

The ocean blue theme trails into the fabrics and rugs of the guest house living room. Comfortable, wide-armed, woven seating and a coffee table offer the perfect place to watch the day wind down, or get together to plan the next.

"NOBODY COULD DENY THAT TO BE A GUEST IN A HOUSE OF MRS. WHARTON'S WAS A DEEPLY, DELICIOUSLY, DELICATELY LUXURIOUS EXPERIENCE."

—Percy Lubbock, *Portrait of Edith Wharton* (1947)

Guests can take a relaxing soak in this tub, surrounded by deep blue Mexican tiles, or shower with full ocean views.

ABOVE: *A stone-sculptured headboard mimics the waves of the ocean and establishes a beach theme in this under-*
stated guest room. No-fuss white cotton bedding and a row of melon-colored pillows encourage a guest to come relax.

OPPOSITE: *Breakfast, lunch, and dinner are served on the waterfront patio, with its endless ocean views. A canopy*
of natural-wood logs—timbers from Santa Fe—absorbs the hot sun and provides shade to diners.

California Dreaming

This little 940-square-foot guest house has an air of grandness that makes you smile. All of the architectural details—the columns, the terrace, the walled and gated garden—make the house seem like a miniaturized version of a home five times the size.

In fact, architect Jim Sneed's inspiration came from the small-town planning concepts he had seen in Florida, where oceanfront homes take up little space, and their structures focus outward more than inward. The big walk-out balcony over the front door is a good example of that.

Located across from the larger, oceanfront main house, this guest house sits on a mere fifty-by-fifty-foot lot. In working out the design details, Sneed used many of the same materials that were used in the main house, as well as bringing in things that suit this East Coast family's taste. They like the fact that it has a little bit of a Nantucket feel. The two woods in the space come together in the kitchen, where there are maple cabinets and countertops, and red oak plank floors.

The owners primarily wanted the guest house for their daughter, who would spend six months at a time here. And when a grandchild was on the way, it was especially important to have the family together. The daughter and her husband worked closely with the architect to review the layout and their needs. The result is a home in which every inch of space is usable. There are storage areas everywhere—under the stairs, under the eaves. There are even doors inside the closets that lead to additional storage in the eaves.

Opening up the main rooms, painting the walls white, and keeping clutter down gives the illusion of more space.

Because it's such a small space, the owners decided to keep the main living area open, as one large room that includes the kitchen and living room.

The home is comfortable and easy to care for. It has a fully equipped kitchen, a washer and dryer, and central air conditioning. With beach-going the primary activity, the owners installed an outdoor shower.

The house has two bedrooms, both with ocean views. The master bedroom has a walk-out balcony and king-sized bed, and the second bedroom has twin beds, a chest of drawers, and bookshelves filled with good reading. Guests can wake up when they like, run off to the beach, and come visit the main house whenever the spirit moves them.

"I NEED SCARCELY TO TELL YOU THAT I AM VERY HAPPY HERE, SURROUNDED BY

EVERY LOVELINESS OF NATURE & EVERY LUXURY OF ART & TREATED WITH A

BENEVOLENCE THAT BRINGS TEARS TO MY EYES."

—Henry James to Mary Cadwalader Jones, October 23, 1904

CHAPTER TWO

In the Spirit of a Time and Place

Sometimes the guest spaces we create are grounded in a specific time or experience we want to share. In this chapter you will tour a collection of these, from Nantucket Island to Santa Fe. The owners have designed guest rooms and guest houses that capture a very specific mood and feel, and sometimes introduce an element of surprise to make you smile. These are spaces that, by their very design, offer an instant escape.

There's the San Diego condominium that is designed to look as though it is an outside street, with each room representing a different country. You will also see an enchanting Japanese teahouse that is tucked into the hills of Connecticut, just steps from an old family farmhouse. And there is the very imaginative Santa Fe guest house complex, where many rooms capture the essence of Santa Fe style, while another, called the spa, is so exotic it could just as well be in Bali.

A Dreamhouse-Come-True

Manhattan interior designer Susan Zises Green had been making the trek to the island of Nantucket for thirty years when she first came upon this sweet little cottage twelve years ago. She distinctly remembers the morning she found this place she refers to as a "little gift box." In fact, she came upon it while meandering through town on her bike. For no special reason, she turned down this particular street and came upon the home. The shape of the house, the plot of land—the whole package—just stopped her in her tracks. And for some reason she just decided to ask if it happened to be for sale. The owners said yes, and before she knew it she was inside taking the grand tour. The cliché of love at first sight could have been defined by this moment in time.

The fact that it was half the size of other homes Susan had seen did not matter. As she moved through the house and saw room after room, each with its own fireplace, she became convinced it had to be hers. The fact that the kitchen also had a fireplace, she says, made her swoon. It brought back fond memories of a house she once lived in that had eleven fireplaces, and for this little home to have so many was irresistible. Built in 1824, it was once home to families who worked on the ships that were an integral part of life on the island.

Susan made an offer on the house that morning, and it was accepted in just twenty minutes. Once she moved in, she kept that kitchen fireplace going all year. Her definition of the

Seating covered in a muted Lee Joffa floral called Hollyhock made its way here via Susan's home in Woodstock, New York. It adds just enough color, while keeping this gathering place serene. Madison, the little dog by the fire, became a popular guest here.

perfect evening would be to have guests helping prepare dinner beside a roaring fire, their wine glasses full. In fact, it wasn't long before she found herself leaving the city for weekend jaunts, as well as spending most holidays here with friends and family. For her guests, Susan has stocked the three guest rooms with current books and magazines, music, a chocolate or two, and fresh water.

When the house behind this one went up for sale, Susan purchased that as well. This little block of Nantucket has become a scrapbook of good times, good food, and much laughter.

The text painted on the wall of the game room was inspired by a reproduction slipware bowl. The names on the wall include the former owners as well as members of Susan's family and her pets.

ABOVE: *Framed botanicals adorn this unusual guest room wall made of cardboard. Susan wanted to create a wall treatment that would complement the heavy Adirondack-style furniture she placed in the room. Her solution was to cut a pattern out of rolled cardboard, hang it like wallpaper, and paint it.*

OPPOSITE: *A white antique iron bed, painted blue dresser, and quilt give this guest room a lighter mood. What looks to be a baby's dress in a frame on the wall is really the paper artwork of Susan's friend, artist Mellie Cooper of Southport, Connecticut.*

Coastal Bliss

This is a house with a very romantic story behind it. Built in 1760, it once sat on a plot of land in New Hampshire. But one day a woman and her husband came upon it while shopping for antiques. Instead of finding a small treasure that could easily travel home with them, they discovered this house, and it caught the woman's heart.

The couple ended up buying the house and moving it to an old estate property they had acquired on the southern Massachusetts coastline. They had the house disassembled: every brick and board was numbered. Then it was trucked and delivered—complete with its original windows, floors, and doors—and put back together like a giant puzzle.

The current owners came along eight years ago and bought it as a summer home. With four guest bedrooms in the main house, a guest house they purchased next door, and a carriage house from the old estate on the property (complete with an old-fashioned sleeping porch), there is plenty of room for friends and family.

Three of the guest rooms have water views. But one looks out on beautiful, mature holly trees and the old carriage house. In winter, when the red berries unlock from their branches, sinking like little rubies into the white snow, the view is enchanting.

All of the guest rooms, says Faith, the hostess, are decorated like the other family bedrooms, and with some working fireplaces, a harried guest can feel as though time no longer matters. Also, each room has baskets or bowls with essentials like

With the addition of the guest house and refurbishment of the carriage house, this couple has created a treasured family compound by the sea.

earplugs, darkening masks, a sewing kit, and toothpaste. And no matter which room guests stay in, they will find an art theme based on family photos that capture their travels abroad. Faith likes the idea of presenting the guests with these visual stories of the family. She feels it is intimate and welcoming.

With the help of her friend, Boston interior designer Charles Spada, Faith hunted down antique furnishings that would be functional and handsome. On various shopping trips she found an antique dressing table from Brussels that doubles as a writing table, an antique wooden chest for storing linens, and an old wood stand painted white for books and magazines. Antique pewter wall sconces and an antique oil lamp recall the period of this home, adding to the romance of this delightful coastal getaway.

ABOVE: *A sun-drenched kitchen and beautiful views from the sitting room give guests an inviting place to come together any time of day. This section of the house was added in the 1930s, and the current family discovered the big domed windows when they were remodeling.*

OPPOSITE: *Delicate floral fabrics and wallpaper—and twin four-poster beds from Faith's daughter's old bedroom—create a room that is pretty and feminine.*

Over the River and Through the Wood

When this family couldn't find a home that had the privacy they wanted, they decided to buy a twelve-acre waterfront parcel and build a house. The only problem was they needed a place to stay in the meantime. Their solution, after talking with Portland, Maine, architect Rob Whitten, was to build a smaller house to live in temporarily, and later use it for guests, who would inevitably visit them year-round.

Whitten drew up plans for a 1,450-square-foot house that would be built and ready for the family in just two months. With its future as a guest house, it was built just far enough from the main house so that each space would have privacy, but be close enough to encourage coming together for cocktails or meals. Style-wise it would feel like an architectural extension of the main house. But in keeping with the guest house concept, it would have tiny, functional bedrooms, small closets, and a main living area where people could comfortably gather.

For inspiration Whitten studied pattern books that discussed, for example, artist's cottages that could be created for just $2,000. The same things that made these successful are the same things he brought to this space. First of all he sited the house so that it has beautiful water and treed views, and would get plenty of sun. It is on a rise in the land where there are two streams; one turns left and the other right, and then they meet before the bay. Guests cross a little wooden bridge over one of them to get to the house. It's a nice touch, setting up an escape, both visually and physically.

A bridge spans the stream that separates the main house from the guest house.

The interior was designed for easy, low-maintenance living for the couple, their two children, and a dog. The main living area on the first floor is an open space, with cathedral ceilings and floor-to-ceiling glass that takes in the picturesque views of woods, water, and the marina, where the lobstermen and their daily catches mark the day's end.

Whitten integrated a mudroom one step down from the main part of the house, and included a bench, a shelf, and pegs for hanging clothes. There is also a covered porch and a screened porch. Logs cut from the site were used as structural columns and add to the rustic feel. He created a staircase to the second floor that leads to the bedrooms and bath, but he situated the master bedroom in its own wing. The other two bedrooms, which were for the children, are off in a second wing.

Bedrooms hold a bed, dresser, chair, and little side table, just like an old Maine camp cottage would. Whitten continued the camp theme by choosing pine board-and-batten doors with a natural finish, and natural trim for windows. He added peeled white cedar post timbers that are exposed in the living space. Floors are made of two-by-six tongue-and-groove spruce decking—big and rugged, and also fitting into the restrained budget. A full basement allowed the family to store their belongings before moving into their new, larger house just across the ravine.

When it's time to prepare a meal, the open kitchen space allows everyone to come together, whether they're cooking, cleaning, or dining. The butcher-block work island that faces the water makes working in the kitchen a pleasure. Cabinets are dark-green laminate, and the cast-iron rolled-edge sink recalls a 1920s summer cottage.

Now that this is a guest house, friends can enjoy all that this family did for two-and-a-half years. They can hibernate, enjoy nature, or run off to nearby Freeport for a shopping spree. The house is set up much like a bed and breakfast these days, with a stocked refrigerator, fresh linens, and quiet places to relax. All the guests have to do is enjoy the light-drenched rooms and beautiful views.

Trees felled from the site infuse a dose of character and nostalgia to the covered porch.

Adopting the layout of old summer cottages, the main living space is one big room. Two stories of windows welcome the sunshine.

> "YOU NEEDN'T BRING SUPPLEMENTARY APPLES OR
>
> CANDIES IN YOUR DRESSING BAG. THE WHARTONS
>
> ARE KINDNESS AND HOSPITALITY INCARNATE."
>
> —Henry James, letter of October 17, 1904

With woods just outside, there's no need for window treatments. The simple wood table and chairs in apple red offer a cheery place to work or dine.

Lakeside Summers Anchor a Family

KEZAR LAKE, NEW HAMPSHIRE

Interior designer Heather Wells has been summering with her family on Kezar Lake, New Hampshire, since she was a young girl. Five years ago they teamed up to rehab this 1890s farmhouse, which can accommodate her siblings, their children, and her parents, who now live here year-round.

During the renovation, all the windows were replaced, except for the row in the eaves, each of which frames and sits squarely behind the heads of the guest beds. The wood floors in the guest rooms are painted for a clean, country flavor. Each room is a different color with unique furnishings, but they all have the same simple components: a quilt folded at the foot of the bed, two needlepoint pillows at the head, an antique hand-hooked rug, painted furniture, a side table, a lamp, and crisp white linens.

Guests are assigned rooms named by their color—there is the pink room, the green room, and so on. Towels are coordinated with the room colors so there is no confusion in the bathroom. When the family turned one bedroom into a bathroom, they kept the old claw-foot tub, and added a glassed-in shower area and two pedestal sinks.

The entire second floor, with its three bedrooms, is devoted to guest quarters. The third floor now has a loft for the youngsters, who can bed down together with their sleeping bags.

An open and screened-in porch that wraps the farmhouse is the perfect place for everyone to get together after a day on the lake.

LEFT: *An antique chest holds good reading, New England artist Eric Aho's cheery yellow painting, and a bouquet of fresh-picked flowers. The decorative ferkin (the maple bucket) evokes the New England theme. Contemporary paintings by Aho and other New England artists bring vivid color splashes to the space.*

OPPOSITE: *The first-floor library gives guests and family members a quiet place to read. The contemporary artwork of New England painter Emily Mason adds brightness to the sand-colored walls, and antique New England baskets add interesting texture.*

Once a bedroom, this spacious bathroom can accommodate a mother bathing a child in the tub, while other family members get refreshed at the double pedestal sinks. Plenty of wall hooks help guests keep track of their bath towels.

Desert Style

When the owner of this Santa Fe property first came here, it was as a guest at a friend's house. After one visit, he fell in love with the landscape and area, and began to hunt for a home of his own. Eventually he decided to rent the guest house, and ended up buying it, the 2,600-square-foot main house, and all five acres they sat on.

He remodeled all of the spaces but one, which he gutted to create an entirely new area he calls the spa. Beyond having a stunning bedroom, it is equipped with a sauna, steam and massage rooms, and an outdoor hot tub. To truly keep the peace here there is no television or telephone.

According to designer and builder Julie Ann (Jae) Larsen of Mad Dog Construction, who created all the spaces here except the main house, it was the spa that gave her the greatest challenge. What began as a concrete slab turned into a place that, when the door closes, takes a weary guest to a new time zone.

From the latilla-covered ceiling to the mahogany-countered massage room, the spa offers an atmosphere where no stress can survive. The latillas—created from tree limbs that are force-grown and then stripped of their bark—emit a soothing yellow glow. Their texture, color, and varying sizes add to the exotic feeling of the space.

A solid wall of glass doors retains privacy but can easily slide open. Floor-length white sheers can be drawn to diffuse the sunlight but are inevitably lifted and tossed by the occasional breeze. Jae put a window in the dry cedar sauna so that guests

Guests can enter this sun-soaked patio with breakfast in one hand and a good book in the other.

95

can take in the dreamy view of a field with a ribbon of blue river. She chose Brazilian slate to wrap the shower, floor, and even the ceiling. A rain-head shower bathes guests in a big wash of water drops, providing the ultimate in relaxation after a massage or a steam. Rather than have a normal drain in the shower, which she finds unattractive, she sloped the slate floor and created a trench of hand-polished black river rock to catch the water. When guests shower, the water disperses and literally disappears into the floor.

Instead of installing an ordinary sink, she designed and built a console with a concrete countertop to hold a striking vessel sink. The faucet emerging from the wall is a sweet metaphor for a natural water source. An antique Indian mirror and a pendant drop-light of art glass bring more color and drama to the space.

Sequoia, a local artist in the area, created a series of candle holders that sit on the wall outside the shower. With a glow from beeswax candles, these provide ambiance for guests padding off to, or coming from, the shower. And for anyone choosing the outdoor Jacuzzi, there's the added treat of music—from Bach to Elvis. Jae thoughtfully hid the sound system from view.

Each of the guest spaces—from the bedroom in the main house, to the studio, to the little casita (a five-hundred-square-foot efficiency apartment)—is different from the others. The fabrics and furnishings are a delightful mix of southwest, Asian, and Indian palettes. What they do share, however, is a laid-back look, which puts guests at ease for weekend or extended stays. Santa Fe, the host says, is a place of great physical beauty, one that is a gift to the senses. This retreat he created for guests is the ultimate gift to them.

The guest bedroom in the spa is all about a Zen-like calm. With its latilla-covered ceiling and cloudlike sheers, this room invites sleep and promotes relaxation. It's the perfect place to nap after a deep-muscle massage.

ABOVE: *When the heat of day subsides, there is no better place for guests to dine than on the outside porch, just steps from their rooms. This is a beautiful place to watch the starry night emerge.*

OPPOSITE: *Here in the casita, a five-hundred-square-foot studio, guests can come and go as they please. The space is warmed by tiles and fabric in punchy desert colors.*

"I DO NOT REMEMBER ANY HOUSE WHERE THE HOSPITALITY WAS GREATER OR MORE FULL OF CHARM THAN AT THE MOUNT. AS ONE THINKS OF IT IN RETROSPECT, THE WORD 'CIVILISED' COMES TO ONE'S MIND."

—Berkeley Updike, quoted in *Portrait of Edith Wharton* (1947)

In this thoughtfully designed spa room, weekend guests can get revitalized, and then walk a few steps to the shower to refresh themselves.

ABOVE: *Candlelit walls and cool, sleek Brazilian slate create an irresistible bath sanctuary.*

OPPOSITE: *With its warm wood accents and stucco walls, this fireplaced guest bedroom in the main house is quintessentially Santa Fe.*

ABOVE: *In this guest bedroom, the spirit of Santa Fe is captured in subtle design accents and carved wood pieces.*

OPPOSITE: *At the end of the day this living room brings guests together in a casual, comfortable setting.*

A Fantasy Condo

The whimsical and unusual design of this condominium was inspired by the owner's desire to create a space that would entertain his guests. The owner thought it would be great fun to have a place that, when guests stepped in, would surprise them with the appearance of a miniature village piazza—complete with lanterns—and where all the rooms represent different places.

For builder and designer Julie Ann (Jae) Larsen, the project became a creative dream. She called on memories and photographs from her own travels to develop the space. In room after room, nothing is what it seems: a coat closet looks like a phone booth; the powder room looks like a public restroom; the dining area looks like an outdoor café. And each room, says the owner, is styled after a particular country. The master bedroom represents France; the guest bedroom, a B & B in Ireland; the dining area, an Italian piazza. What weekend guest would not embrace this fantasy? There is even a home theater, with its four red suede Lazy Boy chairs sunk into a 1930s Art Deco—style room. Jae even installed red velvet curtains for the entry, created a Cinema Paradiso sign, and added an authentic movie marquee to set the stage.

There is a thousand square feet of brick in the condo to maintain the street theme and the fantasy. The design idea, Jae says, was to let visitors first see the obvious, and as their stay goes on, to discover one surprise after another. Two scooters in the garage give guests a fun way to tour the neighborhood, and buzz back here fast to unwind on the piazza.

Lanterns, a brick wall, and an awning all create the illusion of an Italian piazza.

ABOVE: *The home theater has cushy seats that seem to beg for a long love story on screen.*

OPPOSITE: *The kitchen may be the only room in the space with a straightforward design. Open to the main living area, it gives guests and the host the opportunity to be together while food is prepped and cooked.*

Japanese Teahouse

When the two-hundred-year-old family farmhouse, tucked into the hills of a tiny New England town, was getting a bit cramped for family get-togethers, building a guest house seemed the best solution. But it was not to be just any guest house.

Sitting just five hundred feet from the main house, down a path into the woods and adjacent to a stream that tumbles down the side of a hill, is a guest house that resembles a Japanese teahouse. Hidden from view of the farmhouse, the teahouse stands on its own, without having to fight for aesthetic dominance, says Marty, one of the owners. Since she and her husband built it, they have added new pathways through the woods and surrounded the teahouse with a Japanese-style garden.

Before deciding to build the teahouse-style guest house, she thought a log cabin would be the perfect fit. But after speaking with a local architect and touring a few of his small Japanese-style houses, the teahouse idea emerged. Marty has had a lifelong interest in Asian culture, as have three of her children. Her daughter spent two years studying Chinese in Taiwan; one son taught in Japan; and another son majored in Chinese in college and later married a Chinese-born woman.

The teahouse is a small structure of seven hundred square feet, but its thoughtful layout, high ceilings, open living space, and loft make it appear much larger. The loft can sleep two, as can the master bedroom with a king-sized built-in bed. Another guest room has a built-in twin bed, and what is called

The entryway to the space has Shoji screens that can slide closed to offer privacy while still bringing in light.

the "tatami room" has another twin bed. There are several futons for any additional people sleeping over, and plenty of space for them in the main living space and porch. It is a self-sufficient space with a small galley kitchen, soapstone countertops, and an efficiency refrigerator under the counter.

The late builder was a Tibetan Buddhist who lived on a mountaintop in the area, surrounded by an old chestnut forest. Many of the trees here died in a blight one hundred years ago but had not fallen to the ground. The builder took one of these beautiful specimens and brought it into the teahouse, integrating it as an architectural detail in the living room. The flat stones that surround the fireplace come from the same forest.

Many beautiful woods have come together in the creation of this house, among them, fir, cedar, and redwood. When you step into the front door, the smell of the woods is strong in the air. A bench and table were made for the house by the builder from an apple wood tree that came down in the tornado of 1989.

It was important to the owners to have the composition be as natural as possible, both aesthetically and environmentally. So instead of painted Sheetrock walls, which can go up quickly, they built plaster ones, a much more tedious procedure but with an incomparable effect. Being in the woods, the house doesn't get enough sun for a successful solar heating system, but the wood stove has turned out to be the perfect heat source for chilly summer or fall nights. The house gets closed each winter.

A walk through the woods leads to the teahouse, which, while only five hundred feet from the main house, feels very far away.

ABOVE: *This view from the back of the living room reveals the sense of spaciousness created by the open plan. The three massive wood beams that move across the ceiling were carved from tree trunks to fit the space.*

OPPOSITE: *Another guest bedroom sits just off the living room and is partially framed by the ancient tree the builder installed on the wall. The tree, the adjacent stove, and its reaching pipe sit like sculptures in the room.*

"EVERY POSSIBLE AND CONCEIVABLE COMFORT IS PROVIDED

FOR THE BODY—AND EDITH'S BRILLIANT CONVERSATION

IS RICH NOURISHMENT FOR THE MIND."

—Matilda Gay, diary entry about a visit to Ste.-Claire-le-Château,
quoted in William Rieder, "Edith Wharton and the Walter Gays"

*The base of the bed in this tiny guest bedroom doubles as a storage area. Large windows provide a view
of the trees outside. A paper light, rounded window, and slat-styled ceiling embrace the Asian style.*

All Things Desert

~~~~~~

SANTA FE, NEW MEXICO

This Santa Fe area getaway was designed and built with the signature of the owner, an interior designer, all over it. Every room of the 4,100-square-foot home empties into a covered porch, and all the floors are covered in tumbled bricks. She guesses that there could be a total of 33,000 bricks blanketing the floor's surface. In keeping with the region's building tradition, all of the walls are made of mud plaster. Furnishings are an eclectic mix from local establishments, including flea markets. Twenty sets of antique Mexican doors—each one different from the next—distinguish the rooms.

To break up the earthy palette, the owner made each room's beamed ceiling a different color. In one guest bedroom she opted for hand-peeling the beams and keeping them natural. She chose sand-colored walls and crisp white for the bed linens and headboards. Each twin bed is piled with pillows covered in linen shams detailed with delicate rosettes. Great beds, ample closets, and big, heavy doors to keep the noise out are mandatory, she says, as are lofty down comforters and Euros. The rooms are situated so they capture pleasant views. This room has a private patio where guests can venture out in their pajamas and have total privacy. If there's a chill in the air, they can light the outdoor fireplace on the patio. Floors are radiant-heated as well.

The house has a second guest bedroom with a hide-a-bed. The owner says she always spends a night in her guest bedrooms so she can make sure everything a guest needs is there. Her list of essentials includes reading materials, terry slippers and a robe, fresh flowers, soaps, an alarm clock, a pad to write on (she has them custom printed on quality paper stock), and a good pen.

Here is a view of a courtyard window, complete with shutters, which are painted in what the owner calls "cosmic blue." This particular blue is said to keep the evil spirits out of the home. From inside the courtyard dining table, guests can look out at the mountains and desert.

A flea–market find, this hammock is the perfect perch for a
guest with a great paperback novel, or for an afternoon nap.

ABOVE: *The library and TV room blends new and old with the leather couch and antique accents. The earthy palette maintains the relaxed mood of the house.*

OPPOSITE: *Another view of the library shows rustic-styled furnishings and shelving for books and decorative accents. Notice the antique entry door here, one of the twenty the owner collected for the house.*

chapter five

ABOVE: *The owner found this six-hundred-pound nineteenth-century French limestone garden sink at an antique store, with moss growing in it! But she saw through the green, designed and built the stand, and then had the faucets installed on the wall mirror.*

OPPOSITE: *The owner wants her guest bedrooms to be clean in spirit and mellow in mood. This one has a pleasant mountain view and, like other rooms in the house, its own shaded patio.*

THE CORE OF MY LIFE WAS UNDER MY ROOF, AMONG

MY BOOKS AND MY INTIMATE FRIENDS.

—Edith Wharton, *A Backward Glance* (1934), reprinted by permission
of the Estate of Edith Wharton and the Watkins/Loomis Agency

CHAPTER THREE

Simple Pleasures

This chapter looks at a variety of guest spaces that coexist with the locale in blissful simplicity. You will see the guest room and bath I have designed in my own home, located in a little seaside town in Massachusetts. I've seeded the room with many personal items, from old family photos and handmade blankets, to my first water-color painting. My goal was to welcome guests into my life. Then there is Manhattan interior designer Eric Cohler's transformation of a wonderful old antique barn in Connecticut into a guest house that doubles on occasion as a dance studio. Serene country views abound, and an eclectic collection of furnishings and art create a unique atmosphere. Also featured in this chapter are four Canadian lakeside retreats that were designed by two sisters who are also interior designers. Three are old family homes—two boat-houses and one log cabin—that have seen generations pass through their doors. These guest spaces have little to do with formal interior design and more to do with history and people. A new boathouse, though it shows more design intervention, remains simple and true to lake life.

These are all beautiful places in their own way. Each offers guests a place where life as they know it disappears quickly, and gives them memories that linger.

In Cottage Style

Except for a brief New York adventure, my husband and I lived in downtown Boston for more than twenty years before moving here. We searched all over New England, looking for a town with a self-sufficient village. We wanted to be a walk or bike ride from the grocery store or the beach. Ironically, we ended up just thirty-five minutes north of the city in this postcard-perfect village with a beach—one we had visited many years ago when we were in college.

We found and fell in love with this 1931 craftsman-style home with a big front porch, which is now lined with four big white rockers—the perfect spot to watch the Fourth of July parade. It's on a tiny plot of land generously planted with perennials that create an extravaganza of blossoms from spring to late summer.

We thankfully had little to deal with in terms of rehab. In fact, the biggest project in the house was the guest bathroom, which we took back to the studs. The guest bedroom, once painted an electric shade of pumpkin orange, just needed a new paint color, curtains, and furniture.

We had plenty of furniture from our old house, as well as art. The only thing we did not have was a bed for the guest bedroom. While we loved the idea of having an antique iron bed, we decided it was more important to have a queen-sized bed that could accommodate a couple. Also, the couch opens into a twin bed in case a child comes along with mom and dad for a sleepover.

We wanted the guest bedroom and bath to feel like a beach cottage, much like the rest of the house. The walls are painted the palest salmon I could find, a color I felt would complement the space on a sunny day, and give it a pleasant glow on a gray day. The colorful floral quilt and a floral hook rug make the room feel inviting. The curtains are two shades lighter than the walls and have a whimsical

I like to have color come from just a few sources to maintain serenity. Fresh flowers, a vase, photographs of flowers, and my watercolor of a wicker chair in the windowsill seem to be just the right mix.

star pattern. I found the fabric in Boston's Chinatown and made the curtains and ties in just a few hours.

The little side table with a carved shell was once pale salmon. I painted both tables in the room with high-gloss white paint to match the finish on the iron bed. The bigger table—a flea market find that once was dark mahogany wood—holds a collection of old family photos. In a corner opposite the bed there is a chocolate-colored wicker armchair, and a wicker basket on the floor holds two quilts our late mothers knit and crocheted. Until we had this guest room, we had them tucked away. We felt this room, with the rows of old family photos, would be the perfect place to have them come to the light of day.

For additional color and texture, we wrapped the walls with photographs we took while visiting Paris and Giverney. We have about thirty of these throughout the house, all in frames we found at New England flea markets and either reconditioned or painted.

There's a sweet feeling in this room—one that is anchored in memories of people and places, past and present. It is a room we have designed and furnished to make guests feel relaxed and special.

The guest bath is directly outside the room, just across a narrow hall. In redesigning the bath the goal was to recall what a beach cottage bathroom might have looked like in the 1930s. The only thing we kept in here from the original room was the window shutter. We pulled up the tile, removed the sink and tub, and went back to the studs. The floor is now black-and-white tumbled stone with black grout, and looks as though it has been here for a long time. There is a new claw-foot tub that we hope tempts our guests to take a bubble bath, a big showerhead for a lavish wash, a new pedestal sink, and bead-board paneled walls. The walls are all vanilla, and the only color comes from a trio of antique bottles and vases, shells, and sea glass. I've had the blue and orange vases for more than twenty years; I found them up near Lake Winnipesaukee in the window of an antique store. It's very important for me to carry small things like this through life, and keep them in just the right spot to bring back the memory.

Setting the bed under one of two eaves keeps the feeling cozy and offers two distinct views.

ABOVE: *When we put the bead-board walls up we had a choice of narrow or wide caps. We chose the wider cap for its warmth, and I thought it would be perfect for adding shells and starfish. I purposely chose linen curtains with a pattern that looks like streams of water working their way down to the floor.*

OPPOSITE: *These tumbled stone tiles are cool, not cold, on bare feet, and feel velvety. The guest towels are big and extra soft, and I keep bubble bath and other essentials in the vanilla-colored floor cupboard.*

Barn-Inspired

When Manhattan interior designer Eric Cohler first toured this old Connecticut barn, it was a guest house for birds, bats, and beetles, as well as an old car and boat. Built into the side of a hill, the barn once stored grain. When his clients, who own the barn and the large farm it sits on, said they wanted a guest house, Eric suggested this wonderful old structure could serve the purpose.

Soon enough, the barn was gutted and transformed into a dual-purpose structure. Today it serves as a guest house as well as a place for dance practice and recitals. The lower level, which once housed cows, now stores an antique car. The main and loft levels are equipped with a kitchen, living room, bedroom, and bath. The twenty-five-foot ceiling keeps the space open and has a dramatic effect. A cantilevered balcony with French doors sits at the back of the barn and opens the view to the mountains and sunsets.

The first-level floor is sprung maple so it's comfortable to dance on, and the upstairs loft is the perfect size for an orchestra that might be called in for a recital. For dance practice, there are the customary barres working their way around the main room, as well as mirrors to keep the room light and open. These days Eric rents the barn and has found those barres to be the perfect place to display his art collection.

In decorating the space he opted to whitewash the interior walls to keep the look fresh and light, and installed radiant-heated floors. He cut in windows and had the barn insulated.

French doors capped by a stack of eight-by-eight windows reveal the breathtaking mountain views and capture the sunset.

Nearly all furnishings and accents came from Eric's antique hunts in Hudson, New York; Brimfield, Massachusetts; and Sheffield, Massachusetts. He also found items at auctions, on eBay, and at the flea markets on 26th Street in Manhattan.

There is a big ceiling fan that eliminates the need for central air conditioning, and electric shades reduce the sun's heat. To maintain the rustic look, he hid the buttons that control them.

There is a galley-style kitchen with a refrigerator under the counter, a two-burner stove, a microwave, and a tiny dishwasher. The kitchen is equipped to cook for six, Eric says. He created a hidden staircase in the core of the barn so that guests can drive in without having to go outside to enter. The bathroom is on the first floor, designed simply with subway tiles, a pedestal sink, and a wall of mirrors to keep it light. He positioned the bed in the loft so that those sitting up in bed can see the full moon through a window he installed on the other end of the barn.

Eric's advice for anyone creating a guest house is to keep it open and loose; if it feels too precious, he says, guests will just not feel comfortable.

An antique Balinese canoe suspended over a cozy seating area is just one of many ways in which old and new come together harmoniously.

ABOVE: *How thoughtful that the owner installed a window at the opposite end of the barn wall, so that when the moon is full, it fills the frame.*

OPPOSITE: *While the mirrors are here for practical reasons, they also serve to bathe this barn in light. The dance barres allow not only the easy changing of art displays but also a very up-close, personal view.*

Three Lakeside Cottages

Like many pristine lakes in Canada and the U.S., Muskoka Lake is home to a number of cottages that have been built on its shores over time, many of which have remained in families for generations.

Most are not about perfect designs with matching furnishings for the inhabitants or their guests. Rather, they are about creating comfortable gathering places, where the day's canoe adventure can be described on the old screen porch or by the fire. Where chairs may be a jumble of attic collectibles, from grandma's rocker to Uncle Jim's old barn bench, and most everything has a story behind it. In a lakeside cottage, brightly colored paint and fabrics might hide some of time's blemishes.

This particular lake began to get popular in the 1800s, along with Lake Rosseau and Lake Joseph. Back then, steamboats took the tourists in, and they stayed in lodges and inns.

These two cottages have been in one family for many years. One is a converted boathouse and the other, a log cabin, is for guest spillover from the two-bedroom boathouse. Ontario interior designer Elizabeth De Jong helped design the interiors of these two rustic cottages. The spirit of both is eclectic and homespun—with furnishings from antique hunts and home attics, and some made from logs found on the shores of this enchanting lake.

Whimsical pillows the color of gumdrops add splashes of color to this rustic cottage room.

ABOVE: *Guest bedrooms like this one are precious, peaceful places that take in the lake sounds and views.*

OPPOSITE: *A collection of old bottles is as abundant as the summer memories spent in the cottage. African batik drapes were created by De Jong and are joined in the design scheme by fabrics the owner has collected in his travels.*

Just moments from the boat house, this lakeside log cabin
offers guests some space of their own.

A comfortable bed, a writing table, and the sights and sounds of the lake are all that is needed to make this a perfect guest bedroom.

This cottage has been in interior designer Brigid Glancy's husband Michael's family for nearly one hundred years, and the family continues to summer here. Built by his grandparents on its own little island, it comprises a main house and a boathouse for guests. Years ago, before the road was built, the family came here by boat. Everything vacationers needed would come by boat via specialty purveyors, from the man who delivered meat to the bakers. When Michael's grandparents lived here they had a cook, a cow, a vegetable garden, and a launch that the family still uses. The launch is called the Waw Waw 2, which means Wild Goose in Indian—just a suggestion of the wild boat races that have taken place here over the years.

Like other lakeside cottages, this one is full of knotty pine and bead board, along with furnishings that reflect many summers past. The original white enamel kitchen table sits on the original hardwood floor. There's no dishwasher, and why would you want one, when standing here tidying up after a family meal is part of the experience?

The old hickory chairs and table on the porch have been here for as long as anyone can remember. A huge perennial garden, chock full of lilies, hostas, and other colorful blooms, has been coloring the landscape for at least eighty years.

Bedrooms in these old lakeside cottages tend to be built waterside so that guests and family can hear the cry of the loons, and the water lapping underneath the boathouses. When the

The boathouse porch faces the water, as do the favorite guest bedrooms.

guest bedroom curtains needed updating Brigid opted for a sweet print from Laura Ashley's collection. (And by the way, there was no sewing involved. She roughed it with sticky hem adhesive.)

When guests come here to stay, she says, they bring their own linen. That's the custom. Guests get their choice of rooms (family members give up their rooms for guests) and sometimes, Brigid says, there's so much changeover that they call this period musical beds. Children end up in sleeping bags, all together in one room.

After a morning swim guests can count on a big family-style breakfast to begin the day. Often lunch and dinner are prepared on the outdoor granite barbecue. The porch is where everyone really lives in the summers. Instead of a grander, screened-in porch, this one is open, with a roof just to provide shade on the long summer days.

ABOVE: *Another guest bedroom has a view of the woods.*

OPPOSITE: *When the summer breezes move across the lake, there is no better place to enjoy the scenery than on the porch.*

"HERE WAS SUCH A HIGH GOAL OF PERFECTION IN FOOD

AND WINE, IN TALK, BOOKS, OLD FURNITURE, PICTURES,

AND THE ART OF LIVING, THAT TO SAVOUR IT TRULY

EXERTED ONE'S HIGHEST MENTAL FACULTIES."

—Matilda Gay, quoted in *A Charmed Couple: The Art and Life of Walter and Matilda Gay* by William Rieder

Brigid brought in this star-patterned quilt, and the iron bed came from her family's summer place on another island.
She used to sleep in this bed with her twin sister when she was a little girl. When there are no guests, her daughter Amelia sleeps in here.

This new boathouse was built as a summer escape, mostly for the owners who give their guests the main house on Lake Muskoka. However, when it's needed, this separate little oasis is also perfect for long-term guests. The owners wanted to keep it light, airy, and water-oriented. Two boat slips sit beneath the living area, along with a steam room/sauna and wet bar.

ABOVE: *This seating area has a perfect view of the water.*

OPPOSITE: *With the living quarters limited to a 650-square-foot space above the boat housing, interior designer Elizabeth De Jong made it feel larger by painting nearly everything white and integrating light furnishings. In addition to sleeping areas, she fit a fireplace, a living room, a teeny kitchen, and a bath. The head of the bed sits in the water's view, and simple blue-and-white Brunshwig & Fils fabric provides a sun-darkening shade. Accessories are a blend of new, antique, and custom-made.*

Vicente Wolf Guest Room

PALM BEACH, FLORIDA

When interior designer Vicente Wolf is asked to design a guest bedroom, he first asks the homeowners how they want their guests to feel in that room, and what amenities they would like to have available. He thinks it is particularly important that guests feel that their rooms are not part of the house—that these spaces are very individual and that they are similar to the rooms one might find at a wonderful hotel. Vicente selects furnishings, art, and linens, right down to the smallest details like toiletries, flower arrangements for the rooms, fruit bowls, magazines, books, a good reading light, and "wonderful linens!" If someone forgets to pack something, there is no worry; it will be here.

The owner of this Palm Beach home wanted her guest room design to have an international, global point of view, but not so serious that a guest would not feel welcome. The end result is an eclectic room with a sense of fun, warmth, and comfort, all bathed in a sunny yellow palette.

Vicente chose a teak room divider from India to serve as the headboard to the bed, and other similar dividers serve as towel racks in the guest bathroom. The architecture theme continues at the bedside with a porcelain window pane from China that is set atop a sleek blonde Noguchi table. A rustic Burmese chair provides an interesting contrast and architectural rhythm. He topped the bed with a summery beach-themed, multicolored striped bedcover, a custom cotton creation from Anachini.

Here is a guest bedroom that has a sunny, tropical feel, achieved with a simple, imaginative design recipe from Vicente Wolf. Guests who stay at this Palm Beach home will enjoy its free and easy mood.

Vicente Wolf Guest House

~~~~~~

LONG ISLAND, NEW YORK

Located on the North Shore of Long Island, this guest house
dates from the 1800s. The owners called upon Vicente Wolf to
create a guest bedroom that was romantic but tastefully
restrained. He created a light, cheery place with twin iron beds,
each piled high with down quilts and separated by a simple,
contemporary wicker table. An old piece of wrought-iron gate
perched atop the table works as a pretty sculpture.

*Vicente captured the essence of romance in this guest bedroom by thoughtfully infusing it with
elements that recall the past. The iron beds topped with lacy pillows and the sweet iron gate
sculpture at the bedside conjure up the stuff of romance novels.*

Vicente Wolf Guest Room

In this Pound Ridge, New York, guest house there are three bedrooms, each, according to their designer Vicente Wolf, with a different sensibility. Guests can choose among them, depending on their mood.

This one has floor-to-ceiling drapes cocooning the king-sized bed, the plush sand couch, the 1940s coffee table, and the nearby desk. The room is perfect for the owner's clients who visit on business trips: the couch is great for long conference calls, but can serve just as well, after five, for a leisurely call home, cocktail in hand. The curtains black out the stimulating scenery, so that a tired guest can easily catch an afternoon nap.

Here is a guest room that offers guests what they need to conduct business, as well as what they need to escape the day's business.

Vicente Wolf Guest Room

POUND RIDGE, NEW YORK

Navy blue bedcovers, crisp white bed linens, and dark woods characterize this masculine, streamlined room with deco overtones. Because the room has low ceilings there is a more horizontal design plane. The long headboard exemplifies this, and functions perfectly if the twin beds are rolled together to become a king-sized bed.

Vicente's rich fabric selection is a combination of cotton, silk, and wool. The navy bedcovers are wool, as is the headboard. The bed linens are made by Anachini.

Dark navy fabric is the perfect complement to the crisp white linens in this tastefully appointed, masculine-styled room.

Getting Personal

Kim, the owner of this Southern California home, calls this guest bedroom the "yellow room" and aptly so, with the palette seen here. She chose yellow, she says, because to her, yellow is most welcoming to guests. She designed the room to convey a sense of her family's history; this level of intimacy, she says, lets her guests know how special they are.

The old iron bed, once painted hot pink, was found by her mother at an antique store twenty-five years ago. She and her mom stripped and painted it—and it was the bed she and her husband used when they were first married.

The antique bedside table was once used by her father in the waiting room of his dental office, and the blue piece sitting on top is from Kim's wedding china. Other china in this room comes from her grandparents, as well as from flea market adventures. Her mother's doll furniture, and the purse and little chair Kim used as a child are in this room too. In case anyone wonders about them, she leaves little notes underneath to explain their significance. Guests won't find family photos, however, because those, she says, belong in the heart and mind.

The "baseball room," as she has dubbed it, incorporates the 4th of July, Cracker Jacks, and baseball. On the beach level of this Southern California house, it is a more casual, whimsical room. But it comes with a message as well. Kim explains the baseball theme is rooted in her husband's desire to raise their

This is a room that is steeped in family history, but is also fresh and pleasant. A starfish reminds guests that they're beachside.

sons through the lessons of dedication, determination, perseverance, integrity, and friendship. John, now sixteen, and Matt, eighteen, have been bat boys for the Yankees, Cubs, Giants, and Padres, and this room, which used to be theirs, is filled with the mementos from those experiences.

When it became a guest room she decided that, rather than change the theme, she would play it up, using fabrics like blue denim, red corduroy, and ticking. It's a mood, she says, that suggests being happy, and what better feeling to give a guest?

The spatterware bowl is filled with baseballs, and guests can't resist picking them up as they recall their own youths and little league games. There's even an old bleacher seat from Wrigley Field in Chicago that creeks complacently when sat upon, as well as a chair from the locker room at Fenway Park. A collection of vintage Cracker Jack toys in an old cigar box is both playful and nostalgic.

ABOVE: *The antique wooden stand adds warmth to the room and offers a place for mementos.*

OPPOSITE: *Baseball is a fun and nostalgic theme for a guest room. You can almost hear the cheering.*

A Maine Retreat, Family-Style

DIAMOND ISLAND, MAINE

Judy Schultz first came to Diamond Island, Maine, on Thanksgiving. She and her family took the short ferry ride from Portland to the island to see what would someday become their summer home. It was a chilly, bleak day, she recalls, but something about it was also romantic. She was able to see past the abandoned home's woeful condition, its missing roof, and the fact that the kitchen was hanging off the back wall.

This house and others nearby once served as military housing but were abandoned after World War II. This one was built in 1904 and served as an officer's home. The developer, Judy's son-in-law's uncle, was prepared to bring these old places back to life. With Judy's daughters, Hannah and Annie, living on the East Coast, she envisioned that they, and her friends from Kentucky, could all come together here under the blue skies and big water views.

Having no experience living in New England, she at first couldn't imagine how she would decorate and furnish the house. But inspiration soon came from the company Maine Cottage, which produces furniture in "bright, happy colors," she says. Guest rooms were eventually painted, each a different color from the next, and each one had its own special view. And for guests who would eventually stay in the yellow, green, or blue bedrooms, there were always fresh flowers bedside, and sometimes a little pile of pretty sticks Hannah collected on her island walks.

With its bright white floors and yellow walls, this room is a cheerful place for people to come together and dine.

Instead of introducing new furnishings, Judy filled the house with a mix of flea market and yard sale finds, and some orphan pieces from back home. Nearly everything, with the exception of any real antiques, got a fresh coat of paint. Blankets for the old iron guest beds came from flea market hunts as well. There is nothing in the house that can't handle a spill, scratch, or stain. To keep things neat and accessible, there are plenty of wall hooks for clothes and towels in the guest bedrooms and baths. Judy ran hooks along bedroom walls, in back of doors, and in the closets. Fresh towels get rolled and stored in a big copper tub.

Sometimes there are as many as fifteen children and their parents staying here, so keeping the decor simple is essential. A big, old painted dining room table brings everyone together for meals, something Judy loves. Many people who redid their cottages opted to enlarge their kitchens by taking out the pantry, but she decided not to and kept the small fire-placed kitchen as is.

While there is not much to do on the island that isn't grounded in nature, there is a general store, and, as you step off the ferry, there is a four-star restaurant. It is the perfect getaway that's not too far away.

A friend of Judy's decorated the stairwell with hand-painted black-and-white scenes of Diamond Island; old photographs of the island climb the wall.

Judy created understated guest bedrooms that, more than anything, provide her guests with pleasant, colorful escapes.

"I AM THRILLED TO THE SPINE....I FEEL AS IF I WERE GOING TO GET MARRIED—

TO THE RIGHT MAN AT LAST!"

—Edith Wharton to William Royall Tyler, ca. 1921,
on her new home, Chateau Ste. Claire in Hyeres, France

Bibliography

A Charmed Couple: The Art and Life of Walter & Matilda Gay. New York: Harry N. Abrams, Inc., 2000.

de Wolfe, Elsie. *The House in Good Taste.* New York: Rizzoli International Publications, Inc., reprinted 2004.

Gay, Matilda, quoted in William Rieder, *Edith Wharton and the Walter Gays.*

Lubbock, Percy. *Portrait of Edith Wharton.* London: Jonathon Cape, 1947.

Post, Emily. *The Personality of a House.* Funk & Wagnalls Company, 1930.

Wharton, Edith. *A Backward Glance.* New York: Simon & Schuster, 1934.

Wharton, Edith, and Ogden Codman, Jr. *The Decoration of Houses* (Revised and Expanded Classical America Edition). New York: W. W. Norton & Company, 1997.

Marshall, Scott, and John G. Waite Associates. *The Mount: Home of Edith Wharton.* Lenox, Mass.: Edith Wharton Restoration, 1997.

Credits

ACKNOWLEDGMENTS

Rizzoli editor Alex Tart, who loved this idea from the start, and Holly Rothman, who worked with me to make it happen.

Photographer Shelley Metcalf, for bringing much of this book to life, and to my other partners in the art of photography, whose contributions gave this book a wonderful sense of diversity.

Special thanks to the homeowners, architects, and designers for sharing their stories.

Betsy Gammons, for introducing me to photographer Shelley Metcalf's wonderful work (and her).

Art director Sara Stemen, whose design has brought everything together just beautifully.

David Kasabian, my husband, for his support, energy, and art.

Sabrina at Eric Roth's office, Linda LaChappelle, Judy Ito at Ronchetti Design, and Francis Smith of Eric Cohler's office for all of their help.

Staff of the Trustees of Reservations, Beverly, MA: Susan Hill Dolan, Susan Edwards, Craig Henkels, Bob Murray, Dawn Sylvester.

Staff at The Mount, Lenox, MA: David Dashiell; Erica Donnis for sharing her research and passing along all of these wonderful quotes; Pam Kueber; Susan Wissler.

Katherine Fausset, Watkins/Loomis Agency, Inc., New York.

Historic New England/SPNEA: Lorna Condon, Susanna Crampton.

And finally, special thanks to Gloopy, Margaret and Donagh's super dog, for sitting by my side while I wrote this book.

PHOTOGRAPHERS

Michel Arnaud
Arnaud Associates
130 7th Ave. # 105
New York, New York 10011
Tel. 917-544-1969
Pages: 111, 112, 114, 115, 117

David Bohl, Photo courtesy of Historic New England/SPNEA
Page: 6

Kindra Clineff
95 River Road
Topsfield, MA 01983-2110
Tel. 978-887-2272
kindra@kindraclineff.com
Pages: 130, 133, 134, 135

Michael Grimm
10 Bleeker Street # 6A
New York, New York 10012
Tel. 212-982-9496
Pages: 136, 139, 140, 141

Anna Kasabian
AnnaKasabian@hotmail.com
Pages: vi, viii, 7, 8, 11, 14, 15, 180

David Kasabian
DavidKasabian@hotmail.com
Pages: x, 2, 3, 4, 5, 9, 10, 12, 13, 16

Nancy Klemm
nklemm@comcast.net
Pages: ii, 24, 27, 28, 31

Shelley Metcalf
3225 Highview Drive
San Diego, CA 92104
Tel. 619-281-0049
Shelley.metcalf@cox.net
Pages: 32, 34, 35, 36,37, 38, 40, 41,42,44, 46,47, 48, 51, 53, 54, 57, 58, 59, 60, 62, 63, 95, 96, 98, 99, 101, 102, 103, 104, 105, 107, 108, 109, 118, 120, 122, 123, 124, 125, 143, 144, 145, 146, 148, 149, 150,, 152, 153,155, 156, 158, 159, 168, 170, 171

Eric Roth
52 South Main Street
Topsfield, MA 01938
Tel. 978-887-1975
rothaway@aol.com
Pages: 68, 70, 71, 73, 74, 75, 76, 78, 79, 88, 90, 91, 92, 172, 175, 176, 177, 179,

Jamie Salomon
35 Highland Ave.
Portland, ME 04103
Tel. 207-772-3500
Pages: 81, 82, 84, 87

Vicente Wolf
333 West 39th Street
New York, New York 10018
Tel. 212-465-0590
Pages: 160, 163, 165, 166

ARCHITECTS AND DESIGNERS

Ronchetti Design
16083 San Dieguito Rd.
P.O. Box 474
Rancho Santa Fe, CA 92067
TEL. 858-756-1033

Charles Spada
Antiques on 5 & Charles Spada Interiors
One Design Center Plaza
Boston, MA 02210
TEL. 617-951-0008

Kym Billington
CCBG Architects
PHOENIX:
818 North First Street,
Phoenix, Arizona 85004
TEL. 602-258-2211
SAN DIEGO:
2310 Kettner Blvd.
San Diego, CA 92101
TEL. 619-234-2212
Info@ccbg-arch.com
ccbg-arch.com

Jim Sneed
Bokal & Sneed Architects
244 Ninth Street
Del Mar, CA 92014
TEL. 858-481-8244
Jsneed@bokalandsneed.com

Susan Zises Green
Susan Zises Green, Inc.
475 5th Avenue
New York, New York 10017
TEL. 212-824-1170

Rob Whitten
Whitten + Winkelman Architects
37 Silver Street
Portland, Maine 04101
TEL. 207-774-0111
Whittenarchitects.com

Heather Wells
Heather G. Wells Limited
Architectural Interiors
BOSTON:
569 Boylston Street
Boston, MA 02116
TEL. 617-437-7077
CHICAGO:
333 West Hubbard Street #2E
Chicago, IL 60610
TEL. 312-464-0077
hgwltd.com

J. A. Larsen
Mad Dog Construction & Design
5616 Northeast 26th Ave.
Portland, Oregon 97211
TEL. 503-490-1703

Eric Cohler
872 Madison Ave. Ste. 2B
New York, New York 10021
TEL. 212-737-8600

Vicente Wolf
333 West 39th Street
New York, New York 10018
TEL. 212-465-0590
www.vicentewolfassociates.com

Elizabeth De Jong
De Jong Designs
30 DeVere Gardens
Totonto, Ontario M5M 3E7
Dejongdesigns@rogers.com
TEL. 416-544-8980

Brigid Glancy Designs
249 Yonge Blvd.
Toronto, Ontario M5M 3JL
TEL. 416-486-1718

N5-0115

8-10-07